The Prince and the Pauper

MARK TWAIN

Level 2

Retold by Jane Rollason
Series Editors: Andy Hopkins and Jocelyn Potter

Pearson Education Limited
Edinburgh Gate, Harlow,
Essex CM20 2JE, England
and Associated Companies throughout the world.

ISBN 978-0-582-42179-0

This edition first published 2000

9 10 8

Copyright © Penguin Books Ltd 2000
Cover design by Bender Richardson White

Typeset by Pantek Arts Ltd, Maidstone, Kent
Set in 11/14pt Bembo
Printed in China.
SWTC/08

Published by Pearson Education Limited in association with
Penguin Books Ltd, both companies being subsidiaries of Pearson Plc

Acknowledgements:
Photographs © BBC 1975

For a complete list of titles available in the Penguin Readers series please write to
your local Pearson Education office or contact: Penguin Readers Marketing
Department, Pearson Education, Edinburgh Gate, Harlow, Essex, CM20 2JE.

Contents

Introduction

'I have an idea,' said Edward suddenly. He jumped out of his chair. 'Let's change clothes. You can be the prince and I'll be the pauper!'

Two babies are born on the same day into very different lives. One is a prince and one day he will be king. The other is a pauper and he will beg on the streets of London.

Then one day, ten years later, they meet and they change places. For a short time they enjoy it. But then they cannot change back.

That same day, the old king dies. Will a pauper now be King of England?

Mark Twain was born in Missouri in the USA in 1835 into a poor family. He did many different jobs. He worked for newspapers and he worked on the boats on the Mississippi River. He also wrote stories.

In 1867 he went to Europe and the Middle East with some other Americans, and he wrote funny letters home about the journey. He put these letters into a book, *The Innocents Abroad*. It came out in 1869 and people liked it. Then came his most famous book, *The Adventures of Tom Sawyer* (1875). It is about the lives of poor families in Mississippi. Mark Twain wrote a second book about Tom and his friends, *The Adventures of Huckleberry Finn*, in 1884.

The Prince and the Pauper (1882) was Mark Twain's first book about people in an earlier time. He writes about the lives of rich people and poor people. His readers laugh and then cry.

In his later years, Mark Twain had money problems. His books from that time show us an unhappier world. He died in 1910.

Chapter 1   Two Babies

One autumn day in 1537, somewhere in the city of London, a boy was born. His family's name was Canty. They were poor and they did not want him.

On the same day, another boy was born. His family's name was Tudor. They were rich and they wanted him.

The first baby's name was Tom – Tom Canty. Only Tom's mother and sisters talked about him. To them, he was a fine boy.

The second baby's name was Edward – Edward Tudor, Prince of Wales. Everybody talked about Edward. They went out into the streets. They danced and sang. The king had a son!

Chapter 2   The Pauper

Ten years later, a boy ran down a dark little street, somewhere near London Bridge. He had no shoes. His clothes were old. He was thin and dirty. He stopped at an old house and ran up the stairs to the top.

This was Tom Canty and he lived with his family – his father, mother, two sisters and his grandmother. They lived in one room. Tom's father slept in a bed; the others slept on the floor. They were paupers.

John Canty, Tom's father, had no money because he didn't work. And he didn't work because he didn't want to work. Because he didn't want to work, the children had to work. Every day the two girls, Bet and Nan, went out with Tom into the streets. They had to stand by the road for hours and beg for money. 'Please give a halfpenny to a poor child,' they said.

Often it rained. Sometimes it snowed. Usually it was very

1

cold. It was a hard life, but they didn't know anything different.

Some days nobody gave Tom money. When he came home on those days, his father hit him. Then his grandmother hit him. She was worse than his father. After that, they sent him to bed without food. His mother usually woke him in the night and gave him a little bread. Then his father hit his mother and Tom cried.

An old man, a churchman, lived in another room in the same house. His name was Father Andrew and he was very clever. Tom visited Father Andrew every day and listened to his stories about kings and princes.

Tom wanted to be a prince. 'I want to speak well and eat nicely,' he said. 'I want to learn Latin and French because princes speak Latin and French.'

'I can teach you these things,' said Father Andrew. 'I can teach your sisters too.'

Some days nobody gave Tom money. When he came home on those days, his father hit him.

'We'd like to learn,' Bet said, 'but our friends will laugh at us.'

Tom's friends laughed at him, but they liked him. They played kings and princes with him. Some of his friends were his soldiers and he gave them orders. Some of them were lords and he gave them orders too. They played by the river. They swam when it was warm. The river water was very dirty but they loved it. Tom could swim very well.

◆

King Henry VIII was King of England at this time. He was an old man. He had many wives but he only had three children – his daughters, Mary and Elizabeth, and one son. His son's name was Edward.

'Go to Westminster Palace and look at Prince Edward,' said Father Andrew one day. 'He really is a prince and he is the same age as you. When his father dies, he will be king.'

Father Andrew's words on that day were very important, but he didn't know that.

Chapter 3   The Pauper Meets the Prince

The next day Tom was hungry when he woke up. He was hungry when he left the house. But today felt different. He thought about Father Andrew's words and he followed a different road. He walked through the streets of London and outside the city walls. He walked slowly down a long, quiet road, past great houses and beautiful trees. And then he came to the palace – Westminster Palace, the home of the king. A crowd of poor people stood outside, because they wanted to see the rich people. Soldiers with fine swords stood at the great gates.

Tom arrived at the gates and looked at the wonderful building. Fine lords and ladies walked in front of the palace. He looked at their rich clothes. Servants ran here and there. Soldiers stood at the doors. But Tom did not see Prince Edward. The soldiers shouted at him, 'Get away from the gate.' And they pushed him back into the crowd.

From that time, Tom went to the palace every day. He begged on the way, and sometimes a lady gave him a penny. More often, a man gave him a kick.

Then, one day, Tom saw a boy. He looked at the boy's beautiful clothes and he knew. It was the prince! He ran to the gates. He wanted to see the prince better.

'I want to see the prince,' he cried.

One of the soldiers hit Tom. 'Get back!' he shouted.

Tom fell, and the crowd laughed.

But the prince saw and was very angry. He came to the gates on the inside.

'Why did you hit that poor boy?' he shouted at the soldier. 'Open the gates. Bring him in.'

'But, sir . . .' said the soldier. 'He is only a dirty beggar.'

'The king, my father, is king of rich people *and* poor people,' answered Prince Edward. 'Bring in the boy.'

The soldier opened the gates and Tom went in. The prince took Tom inside the palace, up some great stairs, through many fine rooms and into one of the prince's rooms.

'Are you hungry?' he asked Tom on the way.

'I am always hungry, sir,' answered Tom.

When they arrived at the prince's rooms, Edward called a servant to the room.

'Bring food,' he ordered. 'Meat, cake, fruit and bread.'

When the food arrived, Tom's eyes were as big as the plates. He opened his mouth but no words came out. Edward sent the servants away and Tom ate.

'Now, who are you?' asked the prince. 'I see you at the palace gates every day. I watch you from the window.'

'Now, who are you?' asked the Prince.

'My name is Tom Canty, sir. I live with my family in a room near London Bridge.'

'In a room? Do you all live in one room?'

'Yes — my mother, my father, my grandmother and my two sisters. Our room is in Cheap Street. It is quite big and it is very cheap.'

'Why do you all live in one room?'

'Because we are very poor,' said Tom. 'My father doesn't work. I have to beg for money. When I don't bring any money home, he hits me.'

'Your father hits you! I will send my soldiers to your house. They will throw him in prison.'

'No, no, please, sir!' said Tom. 'Think of my mother and sisters.'

'Mm. Perhaps you are right,' said the young prince. 'I have two sisters — Lady Elizabeth and Lady Mary. Lady Elizabeth is very clever and kind, but I don't like Lady Mary. She never smiles or laughs. And she never plays with me. And then there is Lady Jane — my uncle's daughter. She is the same age as me and I like her very much. But I don't know any boys. Do you play with other boys?'

'Yes, of course. We play by the river and we swim. Sometimes we play princes and soldiers. I am always the prince!'

Edward looked out of the window. His face was sad.

'I would like to be a poor boy. I would like to play with other boys.'

He was quiet for a minute. Tom ate a chicken leg.

'I have an idea,' said Edward suddenly. He jumped out of his chair. 'Let's change clothes. You can be the prince and I'll be the pauper.'

So Edward put on Tom's old, thin trousers and shirt.

'I'll wash my face and hands first,' said Tom.

After he washed, Tom's clean face was the same as Edward's. They had the same eyes, the same nose, the same hair. Tom put on Edward's fine clothes and shoes.

Edward looked at Tom. Tom looked at Edward. Now Edward was Tom and Tom was Edward.

'Wait here!' said the prince. 'I am going to be a pauper for an hour. I am going to swim in the river.' He took something round and heavy from the table and quickly put it under a large cup on the highest shelf. Then he ran out of the room.

'What will I do?' shouted Tom.

But there was no answer.

Chapter 4   Cheap Street

Prince Edward ran to the palace gates.

'Open the gates,' he ordered the soldiers. 'Quickly!'

The soldiers opened the gates and Edward walked through them. One of the soldiers hit him hard with his hand.

'Do not give orders to the king's soldiers, boy!'

Edward fell to the ground and the crowd laughed. He got up and looked at the soldier. He was a small, thin boy but he looked into the soldier's eyes.

'I am Prince Edward, Prince of Wales!'

'And I am the King of England,' said the soldier.

'You will go to prison for that!'

The crowd laughed again, louder this time.

'Bow to your prince,' Edward shouted at the crowd. He pushed his way through them. His face was red and angry.

'He's mad,' said a man.

'Let's follow him,' said another man.

'No. Mad people are dangerous.'

Edward walked down the road. Nobody followed him. He was angry and he forgot about the river. He came to the city walls and went through the gates into the streets of London. He did not usually walk anywhere, but now he had to walk. Tom Canty never wore shoes, but his feet were hard. Now Edward had no shoes and his feet hurt.

◆

That evening, Edward was very tired and hungry.

'Where can I find food?' he thought. 'Where can I find a friend?'

A man went past him on a horse. Edward called to him, 'Sir! Look at me! Do you know me? Please help me. I am Edward, Prince of Wales, King Henry's son. Please take me back to the palace.' But the man did not listen. He never gave money to beggars.

Then Edward came to King's Hospital.

'Ah! I know this place. My father built this school for poor boys. They will help me.'

Boys played in front of the building. They all wore the same clothes. They ran and jumped. They fought.

'Hey!' called Edward. 'Boy! Bring your teacher here. I am Prince Edward. I want to speak to him.'

The boy laughed. Edward did not laugh. 'Go now!' he ordered, and he hit the boy.

The boy called to his friends, 'This boy is mad. He wants a fight. Let's throw him in the water for the horses.'

So four boys threw Edward into the water. They laughed when he climbed out.

'It is late,' thought Edward. It was nearly dark. 'Where can I sleep tonight? I'll go back to the palace tomorrow.' Then he thought of Tom's house.

'I remember!' he said. 'It was in Cheap Street. I have to find Cheap Street. Tom's mother and sisters are kind – they will help me.'

He walked and walked. Everybody knew Cheap Street, and they showed him the way. The sky was black now. Lights shone in the windows of the house.

Suddenly a heavy hand came out of a dark doorway and took Edward's arm.

'So, Tom Canty! You remember your poor family? What are you doing out at this time? Where is the money from your day's work? Or were you very busy with your friends at the palace? Give me my money!'

'Ow! You are hurting me,' said Edward. 'Are you his father?'

'*His* father? I am *your* father, you stupid boy.' He hit Edward very hard.

'No, no,' cried Edward. 'I am the prince. I really am Prince Edward. Your son, Tom, is at Westminster Palace. He is wearing *my* clothes and I am wearing *his* clothes. We changed places. Can't you see? I am not him. Take me to the palace and bring him home.'

John Canty looked at the boy. There was no love in his eyes. Edward was afraid.

'You and your mad talk! That old man, Father Andrew, puts these stupid ideas in your head. I will kill him one day.'

He took Edward's arm and pulled him down the road. He was a very strong man.

'You can start work early in the morning – at six o'clock. I want two days' money tomorrow.'

Chapter 5   Westminster Palace

And where was Tom Canty? He stood in the prince's room in Westminster Palace and looked at the beautiful things there – fine chairs, pictures of kings and princes, plates of fruit, fine glasses and cups, tall clocks, great swords. He walked round the room in his fine prince's clothes. He tried the great chairs. He took out the prince's beautiful sword.

John Canty looked at the boy. There was no love in his eyes.

'This will make a good story for my sisters,' he thought. 'Tom Canty, Prince of Wales – for five minutes!' But it was longer than five minutes. Tom waited and waited. But Prince Edward did not come back. Now Tom started to feel afraid.

'Where is Edward?' he thought. 'Why doesn't he come back? Somebody will find me. They will ask me questions: "Who are you? What are you doing here? Where is Prince Edward?" They will put me in prison. How can I get out of the palace?'

Then he thought, 'Perhaps I can walk out. I will walk quickly to the palace gates. The soldiers will open the gates and I can run home.'

So he opened the door. Four servants stood outside the door, two on the left and two on the right. They bowed.

'Oh!' cried Tom. He ran back into the room and shut the door.

'That was strange!' said one of the servants.

'Perhaps the prince is ill,' said another servant.

'Let's call Lady Elizabeth or Lady Jane,' said a third man. 'And let's tell Lord Hertford.'

◆

The door to the prince's room opened, and a beautiful girl with a kind face came into the room. Tom looked at her from behind a chair. She was the same age as Tom. He came out and bowed.

'What is wrong, my prince?' she asked. 'Why are you bowing?'

'Help me, help me!' cried poor Tom. 'I am not Prince Edward. My name is Tom Canty. I am a pauper and I would like to go home.'

The girl listened to these strange words with wide eyes. 'Perhaps you are not feeling well, my prince.'

'No, no. You don't understand. Prince Edward and I changed places. He is wearing my poor, thin beggar's clothes and I am wearing his fine, rich prince's clothes. But where is he? Please find the prince and get my clothes back.'

'Come with me,' said Lady Jane kindly. 'Your father wants to see you.'

'My father? Is John Canty here?' asked Tom. But Lady Jane did not answer him.

He followed her through many great palace rooms and then they came to a large bedroom. There was a great bed in the centre of the room. A very large man sat in a very large chair next to the bed. His face was grey and he was ill. When he saw Tom, he smiled weakly.

'What is the problem, Edward?' he said. 'Are you ill? Lord Hertford tells me that you are not well.'

'Are you the king, sir?' asked Tom. He was afraid.

'Of course I am the king. Don't you know your father?'

Tom bowed. 'Your Majesty*, I am not your son. I am not the prince. I am only poor Tom Canty of Cheap Street–'

'Tom Canty? Cheap Street? What are you talking about? Do you think that I don't know my only son?' answered the king angrily. 'You are Edward, Prince of Wales, son of King Henry the Eighth, King of England. Don't make me angry.'

'No, Your Majesty,' said poor Tom.

'I know that you sit for many hours each day with your books and your teacher. Those languages – Latin, Greek, French, Spanish – are difficult.'

Then the king asked Tom a question in Latin. Tom answered in Latin.

The king turned to Lord Hertford and laughed. 'How many paupers speak Latin?' he asked.

Next he asked a question in Greek. Tom did not answer – Father Andrew did not know Greek. 'Very strange,' said King Henry to Lord Hertford. 'He remembers his Latin but forgets his Greek.'

*Your Majesty: You use these words when you talk to a king.

12

'Of course I am the king. Don't you know your father?'

Then he spoke to Tom again. 'You are tired and you are not well. Get some sleep before the banquet tonight. Many great men will be there. They will want to speak to their prince. You will be their king when I am dead. Go now with Lord Hertford. Sleep for an hour, and you will feel stronger.'

Lord Hertford was the king's closest friend. He took Tom back to the prince's room and then he went to the king again.

'My Lord Hertford,' said the king, 'I know that I don't have much time. But I have a lot of work before I die. Get the Great Seal and we will begin.'

'Yes, Your Majesty,' said Lord Hertford. 'I think that you gave the Great Seal to Prince Edward yesterday. I will go and get it.'

'You are right. Yes, yes. Be quick, man.'

But Lord Hertford came back without the seal.

'Your Majesty,' he said. 'The prince can't remember ... He says that he doesn't have the seal.'

'He can't remember!' For a minute the king could not speak. 'Then he really is ill. Nothing is more important to the King of England than the Great Seal. When he is better, he will remember.'

Chapter 6   The King's Boat

There were stairs from the Palace of Westminster down to the River Thames. Soldiers stood on the right and left of the stairs. The people of London were out on the streets by the river. They wanted to see the king's boat and the other fine boats. Tonight was the Prince's Banquet at the Guildhall, about a mile down the river.

The water shone with the colours of the boats, the crowd and the lights. At the bottom of the stairs, the king's boat waited.

Suddenly the great doors of Westminster Palace opened.

14

Everybody was quiet. Lord Hertford came out first. Other lords and ladies followed. They stood on the stairs. And then Tom came out.

'Oooh!' said the crowd. And then they shouted, 'Long live★ Prince Edward!'

Tom wore white. When he saw the river, he nearly cried. He thought about his games in its dirty water with his friends. He walked slowly down the stairs to the king's boat. All the lords and ladies bowed. Lady Elizabeth and Lady Jane followed him into the boat.

Tom stood at the front of the boat, and it moved slowly down the river to the Guildhall.

'Long live Prince Edward,' people shouted when he went past them. The great and rich men and women of London waited for him at the banquet.

'How will this end?' thought Tom.

Chapter 7   Edward Gets Away

John Canty took Edward's ear and pulled him down the street. People laughed when they saw the big man and the small boy. A crowd followed them.

'That's right,' shouted an old woman. 'Teach the boy a lesson!'

But when they came to John Canty's house in Cheap Street, an old man with white hair suddenly stood in their way.

'Don't hurt the boy!' he cried.

John Canty did not answer the old man. He hit him hard on the head. The old man fell to the ground. Then John Canty pulled Edward into the house, and the crowd went away.

★Long live …!: People say this when they want a king or prince to live for a long time.

15

The old man on the ground did not move again. He was dead.

John Canty kicked the door of his family's room and it opened.

'There,' he said to his wife. 'There is your dear son. How much money do you think that he has got for us? I will tell you. Not one penny! And now he is mad, too. Listen to this.' Canty turned to Edward. 'Boy, who are you?'

Edward looked at him angrily. '*I* give orders, not you. But I will answer you. My name is Edward, Prince of Wales.'

Nobody spoke for a minute. Then the old grandmother laughed loudly. Her son laughed too. But Tom's mother and sisters ran to him.

'Oh, my poor boy,' said Tom's mother. She looked at the cuts on his face and feet. She put her arms round him. 'You are always reading and learning. Why didn't you listen to your mother? Your books are making you ill.'

'Please don't cry, Mrs Canty. Your son is well. He is at Westminster Palace. Take me there now and we will find him.'

'Oh, poor child! I am your mother. I love you. Don't say these things.'

It was not funny but Tom's grandmother laughed again.

'Poor child! Hah! *I* am poor, not him. He never thinks about his poor old grandmother. Here I am at the end of my life – a life of hard work. I only want a little drink sometimes. I am not asking for much. And then he comes home with no money.'

'No money – no food,' said John Canty to Edward, and he pushed him hard to the floor.

Suddenly somebody called from outside the room. 'John Canty! Quick! Open the door.'

'What is it now?' said Canty.

'You hit old Father Andrew.'

'And? He wanted to take my son.'

'He is dead. You killed him.'

'Dead?' repeated John Canty. 'I killed him?' He turned to his wife. 'This is bad for us,' he said. 'A lot of people saw me. I am a dead man ... Quick! Take the girls and meet me at London Bridge. I will go a different way with the boy.'

'And me?' cried the old grandmother. But nobody listened to her.

Canty pulled Edward by the arm through dark little streets. They came to the river and saw crowds of people. Fires and lights lit the sky.

'What is happening?' Canty asked a man. 'What are you waiting for?'

'Don't you know? We are going to see Prince Edward in the king's boat, of course. There is a banquet at the Guildhall tonight. Here, have a drink,' said the man, and he gave John Canty a cup.

Canty took his hand from Edward and drank. Edward ran between his legs and away, faster than the wind.

'Hey!' shouted Canty. 'Stop him. Stop the boy. Catch him!' But there was a great shout, 'Long live Prince Edward.' Nobody listened to John Canty.

Edward ran quickly. 'To the Guildhall!' he thought. 'There I will find Tom and we can change places again.'

Chapter 8   At the Guildhall

The richest and greatest men and women of the city of London sat at the long tables in the Guildhall. Tom came in and everybody stood up. They bowed. Tom took his place at the highest table. Lady Jane and Lady Elizabeth sat next to him, and the banquet began. Servants brought wonderful food to the tables. People talked and laughed. There were singers and dancers. Tom started to enjoy it.

◆

Tom took his place at the highest table.

Edward found his way to the Guildhall. He was tired and dirty. But when he saw the soldiers at the great doors, he felt strong again. He looked into their eyes.

'I am Edward, Prince of Wales. Open the doors! I want to come in.' The soldiers laughed. 'I order you! Open the doors!' shouted Edward.

'Get back, you stupid boy,' said one of the soldiers. He pushed Edward away.

'Do you want to go to prison?' shouted Edward. The crowd started to get angry.

'Take the boy away. He is mad,' they shouted. 'We want to see the prince at the end of the banquet. Go home, boy. Go away!'

'I will not go away. I am Prince Edward. That boy in there is a pauper, not a prince. *I* am the son of King Henry.'

The crowd started to look dangerous, but Edward did not

run away. Then a man came out of the crowd and stood next to Edward.

'Perhaps you are a prince; perhaps you are not,' said the man. 'Perhaps you are mad; perhaps you are not. But you are a strong boy and I like you. I will help you.'

'And who are you, sir?' asked Edward.

'My name is Miles Hendon. I am one of the king's soldiers. I arrived back from France yesterday. I am on my way to my country house.'

The crowd came nearer. Now they were very dangerous.

'Stand back!' cried Miles Hendon. He took out his sword and held it up.

'Kill them!' cried somebody from the back of the crowd. People started to throw things. Something hard hit Edward and he fell. Miles stood in front of him and fought the angry crowd. But the crowd was big and Miles was only one man.

'This is not looking good,' laughed Miles. 'I fight in France for my king and country for seven years. Then I come home and a London crowd wants to kill me!'

But suddenly everybody stopped shouting. They heard the sound of horses. A soldier cried, 'Stand back! The king's First Lord is coming past!'

The soldiers pushed the crowd back. Lord Hertford climbed down from his horse and ran up the stairs to the doors of the Guildhall. The soldiers opened the doors and he went in to the great dining room.

Lord Hertford went to Tom and bowed to him. 'Your Majesty,' he said. 'I am sorry. The king, your father, is dead.' Then he stood up and shouted to the people. 'The king is dead. Long live the king!'

And everybody at the banquet shouted, 'Long live King Edward!'

◆

19

Miles Hendon took Edward's arm. They ran away into a dark street and nobody saw them.

Chapter 9   Edward, King of England

Miles had a room near London Bridge. He took Edward there. They heard shouts in the streets behind them, but they did not understand the words. Then the shouts came nearer. 'King Henry is dead!'

Poor Edward! He thought of his father. Henry was a difficult man, but he was always kind to Edward. And Edward was not with him at the end. The boy started to cry. He thought of Lady Elizabeth and Lady Jane and he wanted to be with them.

Then they heard more shouts. 'Long live King Edward the Sixth!'

When he heard those words, Edward felt strong again. 'So now I am king,' he said quietly.

'Prince or king,' said Miles, 'you can stay here with me tonight.'

But suddenly a man stood in their way.

'So you are here,' said John Canty. He took Edward's arm, but Miles Hendon put the boy behind him. He stood face to face with John Canty.

'Who are you, sir? What do you want with this boy?'

'He is my son.'

'*Are* you his son? Do you want to go with this man?' Miles asked Edward.

'No, no. He isn't my father. I will die before I go with him.'

'Then you will not go with him,' said Miles.

'Oh, but I think he *will* come with me,' said John Canty.

Miles put his hand on his sword. 'Do you want to feel my sword? It killed many men in France. It works in England too.'

Canty moved away and they could not hear his words.

'Go!' shouted Miles. 'And never come near the boy again.'

Miles took Edward up to his small room. There was a bed, two chairs and a table.

Edward fell on the bed. 'Call me when the food is ready,' he said.

Miles laughed. 'Yes, "Your Majesty",' he said. 'I will order a banquet from your servants.' But Edward did not hear him. He was asleep.

Miles went down to the kitchen and brought food up to the room. He woke Edward.

'Your banquet is ready, Your Majesty,' he said. 'Come and eat.'

Edward washed his hands and sat down at the table. Miles sat down too.

'Wait!' said Edward. 'Stand up. I am your king. Wait for my orders.' Miles stood up. 'Now, please sit.'

Miles smiled and sat. They started to eat.

'Now, Miles Hendon,' said Edward. 'Tell me about your life.'

'Well, my home is Hendon House, in Kent. My father is Sir Richard Hendon, a rich and important man and a friend of King Henry. He is a good man. I have a younger brother, Arthur. He is very different from my father.

'Arthur wants Hendon House and my father's money. He also wants Lady Edith, but she is my love. So Arthur told my father bad stories about me. My father did not listen to me and he sent me away. And now, seven years later, I am in England again and near Hendon House, my family and Edith.

'I know that my father will be happy. We will be friends again when he sees me. But I do not think that Arthur will be very happy.'

'I will not be kind to your brother,' said Edward, when he heard this story. 'He will have to leave Hendon House. You are good to me and I will look after you well. Give me your sword.

Bow to your king. I name you, Sir★ Miles Hendon! Now you are one of my men.'

After their dinner, Edward fell asleep again with his head on the table. Miles carried him to the bed.

'Poor boy!' he said. 'He has funny ideas in his head. Sleep will be good for him. Perhaps tomorrow he will remember that he is a pauper and not a prince.'

◆

The next morning, when Miles woke up, he looked at Edward in the daylight. The boy's clothes were very dirty.

'I think that I will buy my prince some new clothes,' he said, and he went out.

When Miles came back an hour later, he went into his room. But where was Edward? Miles ran down the stairs and asked one of the servants.

'A young man came here,' answered the servant. 'He said to me, "Tell the boy this. Meet Miles Hendon in Southwark. Come quickly!" So I told the boy and he went. I think the young man's name was Hugo.'

'That man, John Canty!' thought Miles. '*He* sent this Hugo. The boy is in danger.'

Miles took his things and paid for the room. He got his horse ready and started on his way to Southwark.

Chapter 10   A King's Life

Tom woke up in a large bed in Westminster Palace. For some minutes he did not move or open his eyes. Was he back in Cheap Street? When he opened his eyes, he looked for his mother and

★Sir: a name for an important man; a king can give this name to people.

his sisters. But he did not see them. He saw two servants at the foot of the bed.

Tom shut his eyes again quickly and went back to sleep. Wonderful ideas came into his head. He was in a wood in the country and the sun shone through the trees. A small woman came out from behind a tree. She had long red hair and wore a tall hat.

'I know you,' she said to Tom. 'You are a good boy. Your life is very hard. I will help you. Come to this place every week on Mondays. Find this tree. At the bottom of this tree you will find twelve new pennies. Take them – they are yours.'

And suddenly she was not there. In his sleep, Tom ran back to Cheap Street with his beautiful pennies.

'Every night I can give Father one penny,' he thought. 'He will think that I begged for it. He won't hit me. I will give one penny every week to Father Andrew. And I will give the other pennies to Mother, Nan and Bet. We will not be hungry. We will not have to beg.'

And in Tom's sleep, his life was good and he had no problems. Then words came into his head. They got louder and louder. His eyes opened.

'Your Majesty ... YOUR MAJESTY,' said the first servant. 'It is eight o'clock.'

'When Your Majesty is ready ...' said the second servant.

'Ready for what?' asked Tom.

'When you want to get up, Your Majesty...'

'Yes, yes,' said Tom. 'Where are my clothes?'

One servant brought Tom's underclothes into the room and gave them to a second servant. The second servant gave them to a third servant and the third servant put the underclothes on Tom. Next, the first servant brought a white shirt. He gave it to the second servant. The second servant gave it to the third servant. And he put it on Tom. In this way they dressed Tom in his fine

23

clothes. Nearly an hour later, he was ready.

Some different servants brought breakfast. One servant carried the food into the room. He gave it to a second servant. The second servant gave it to a third servant and the third servant put it on the table. A fourth servant put some food on Tom's plate. Two more servants stood behind Tom's chair. They did everything for Tom – or nearly everything. They did not eat the food for him.

After breakfast, a servant said, 'Lord Hertford would like to speak to Your Majesty.'

Lord Hertford came in and bowed. 'Is Your Majesty ready? The men are waiting in the Great Room.' Tom followed Lord Hertford to the Great Room. There he sat in the king's chair.

A man began to talk about money. 'There is no money, Your Majesty,' he said. 'King Henry used all of it. You have twelve hundred servants and you have to pay them.'

Tom spoke. 'We can move to a smaller house. We can live with twelve servants, not twelve hundred. There is a nice house in the city near Cheap Street–'

Lord Hertford took Tom's arm. Tom stopped speaking and his face went red.

A second man bowed. 'Your Majesty, King Henry wanted to give eight hundred pounds to Lord Hertford's son. He also wanted to make him a Lord. Can you write your name here on this paper?'

Tom wanted to say, 'Let's pay the servants first.' But again he felt Lord Hertford's hand on his arm. He did not speak and he wrote his name.

Men came and bowed. They read from long papers for hour after hour.

'I'd like to swim in the river. I'd like to play ball with my friends,' thought Tom. But he did not say that.

Lunch was in the great dining room. There were hundreds of servants. They ran in and out with plates of food. The food was

He sat in the king's chair.

wonderful, but Tom did not enjoy it. He thought only about the beautiful dirty water of the River Thames.

After lunch Tom had a happy hour with Lady Elizabeth and Lady Jane. But they were quieter than they usually were. Their father, King Henry, was dead. At the end of the hour, Tom had to visit his older sister, Lady Mary. She was not friendly and he did not enjoy the conversation.

Tom went back to Prince Edward's room. He sent everybody out of the room. But after a minute or two, a boy came into the room. He was about twelve years old.

'And who are you?' asked Tom.

'Then they are right, Your Majesty,' answered the boy. 'You *are* ill. I am Oliver. Oliver Carpenter. When you make mistakes with your Greek, your teacher gets angry. But nobody hits the Prince of Wales, so he hits me. That is my job. But now you are king, and perhaps you will stop studying. I will lose my job, and my poor mother and sisters will have no food and no home. And we will all have to live on the streets–'

'Stop!' cried Tom. When he understood the boy's problem, he laughed loudly. 'Listen, Oliver Carpenter,' he said. 'I will not stop my studies. I will make many, many mistakes and they will pay you three times more than before! And you will have your job for life and your sons will have the job after you.'

'Oh, thank you, Your Majesty.'

When Oliver stopped thanking Tom, Tom asked Oliver many questions. He learned a lot about Edward's life.

Then Lord Hertford came for Tom and took him back to the Great Room. Tom was different now, he thought.

'You remember more, Your Majesty,' he said. 'You are feeling better; I can see that.'

All afternoon Tom wrote his name on paper after paper. It was not his name, of course – it was Edward's.

And then it was time for dinner!

At the end of the day, Tom went to bed. 'Is every day the same?' he thought. 'The clothes are beautiful, the house is beautiful. The food is wonderful . . . but Cheap Street is better.'

Chapter 11   Stop that Boy!

Edward looked at the young man. He did not like him. The man's eyes were cold and unfriendly.

'Who sent you?' Edward asked.

'Miles Hendon.'

'What is your name?'

'Hugo.'

'What did Sir Miles say?'

'He said, "I am in Southwark. I have hurt my leg in a fight. I can't walk. I want help."'

'Then I will go to him. He is my servant and my friend.'

The young man took Edward out into the country. They walked and walked.

'Where is Sir Miles? Where is Southwark? It is nearer to London than this. How did he get here?'

'We are nearly there,' said Hugo. 'He is in a house in that wood.'

They went into the wood and walked through dark trees. Edward started to feel afraid. They came to a small house. Hugo opened the door and Edward went in.

'So here you are, my dear son!' Edward felt ill when he heard those words. It was John Canty! 'So you want to help your poor dear father.' Canty's smile was ugly and now he was angry. 'I have to live here in these dark woods because I killed that stupid old man. And that was because of you and your games! You want to be a prince and speak Latin and French. Hah! My stomach is hungry and my mouth is dry.'

'Where is Sir Miles?' said Edward. 'Take me to him.'

The food is wonderful . . . but Cheap Street is better.

'You are more stupid than I thought, boy. Your friend Miles Hendon is not here. We used his name. Now, it is time for work. You and Hugo, go and get money. Tom, you beg with your pretty face. Hugo, you watch him. Then buy food and drink – don't forget the drink – for your father. Bring it back here. And be quick.'

Hugo took Edward through the wood. They came to a road.

'This is the plan,' said Hugo. 'You stand here by the road and I sit here. When somebody comes, you talk to them. You say that I am your brother. I am very ill. I am dying, and we haven't any food or money. Ask for help . . . Quick. Somebody is coming now.'

'Oh! Oh! I am dying,' Hugo shouted. 'Bring me water! I am thirsty. I am hungry. Help!'

A man came past them on a horse. He got down when he heard Hugo's cries. 'Poor young man,' he said. 'Can I help you?'

'Kind sir,' said Hugo, 'please give my brother a penny. He can buy food for me.'

'But you are ill. We cannot leave you here by the road. Your brother and I can take you to your house.' He turned to Edward. 'Come here, boy. Let's carry him to your house.'

'I am the King of England,' said Edward. 'He is not my brother. He is a beggar. And he is not ill.'

The man looked at Hugo. 'Hah! So that is your game. You come with me. We will find a nice room in a prison for you. You can get better there.'

Hugo jumped up and ran away into the trees. The man got back on his horse and went away. Edward walked down the road. 'I hope this is the right way to London,' he thought. 'And I hope I never see John Canty or Hugo again.'

But suddenly Hugo jumped out from behind a tree. He caught Edward's arm.

'So, I have to go to prison because of you?' said Hugo. 'Don't you know that they kill beggars? They cut off their heads. I will not forget this, Tom Canty, and I will teach you a lesson.'

They walked under the hot sun. Then they came to a town. It was Friday and the town square was very busy. Old women sold vegetables and bread. Young men sold fish and meat. Hugo and Edward felt very hungry.

There were a lot of people in the square. A woman came past them with a large bag. She had a fine, fat chicken in her bag. She wanted to buy some vegetables and she put down her bag for a minute.

Suddenly Hugo came up behind her and took the chicken from the bag. He ran quickly to Edward and put the chicken in Edward's arms. Then Hugo shouted to the woman. 'Look! That boy has your chicken. Stop him!' And he ran away down a back street.

The woman turned. She looked at her bag and then she saw Edward with her fine, fat chicken.

'Stop that boy!' she cried. 'He has got my bird.'

An angry crowd caught Edward. 'Let's finish him,' shouted one man. 'Kill him!' shouted a woman. 'We kill thieves.'

Was this the end for poor Edward? He heard the sound of a horse – and there was Sir Miles Hendon!

'Help me, help me!' he cried.

'So here you are,' said Miles. 'What is happening here?' The crowd stood back.

'This woman says that I took her chicken,' said Edward. 'But *I* didn't take it. It was Hugo–'

'Ah,' said Miles. 'That is a fine bird.' He spoke to the woman, 'I said to my young servant here, "We want a fine bird." And he has got one.' Then he turned back to Edward. 'But did you ask the good woman first?' Edward did not answer.

Miles took the woman's arm and spoke quietly to her. 'My servant is very young. He is mad. He thinks that he is the King of England. Please don't be unkind to him. Let's look in your bag. Is the money for the chicken in there? Ah, yes.' Miles showed the

It was Friday and the town square was very busy.

woman some money in his hand. 'He is paying you well.'

The woman looked at the money. It was a lot of money for a chicken. She smiled.

'All right,' she said. 'Take the bird.'

'Come, boy,' Miles said to Edward. He pulled Edward up behind him on his horse.

'How did you find me?' Edward asked him.

'I met a man on the road. He told me about two beggars. One of the beggars said to him, "I am the King of England!"'

Edward smiled – but only for a minute. 'Where are we going now?'

'To Hendon House.'

'I will come with you. But after that we will go to Westminster Palace. My people are waiting for me.'

Chapter 12   Hendon House

The next afternoon, Miles and Edward came to a high place. Miles stopped the horse. The sun shone and the sky was blue. They looked down at a small village, a church and a big house with gardens and trees round it.

'There,' said Miles. He smiled. 'My home! The biggest house in Kent. We have fifty rooms and twenty servants. Think of that, Edward!'

They came nearer. 'There is the village,' Miles said. 'Here is our church. And look at that beautiful tree – the best tree in Kent. I often climbed to the top early in the morning. Over there is the river. I played there with my friends when I was a boy. Everything is the same.'

They went through the big gates.

'And this is Hendon House,' said Miles. 'They will be happy when they see me.'

Miles got down from the horse. Edward jumped down after him. Then Miles ran into the house.

A young man sat at a table in the dining room.

'Arthur!' Miles cried. 'I am home. Say that you are happy about that! Where is father?'

The young man looked at him with cold eyes. 'Who are you?'

'Don't you know me? I am Miles Hendon, of course – your brother. I am home from France. I am seven years older, but I am the same brother!'

'My brother died in France. We had a letter from his friend.'

'No, no, I am here and well,' said Miles. 'Where is Sir Richard, my father? He will know me.'

'Sir Richard is dead. He died two weeks after the letter came.'

'No!' Miles sat down suddenly. 'Why didn't you write and tell me?' He loved his father and he wanted to be friends with him again. Then he said, 'Call the servants. They knew me when I was a boy. They will know me now.'

'The servants are new. They all started to work here after Sir Richard died.'

'Now I understand. You sent the servants away. You wrote the letter. You want the house and the money. But your plan will not work. Lady Edith will know me. The people in the village will know me.'

'Lady Edith knows that Miles Hendon is dead. She saw the letter. Next month she is going to marry me.'

Miles jumped up and ran round the table. 'You take my house. You take my money. And now you want to take Lady Edith. I will kill you.' He threw Arthur to the floor and jumped on him. He kicked him hard.

'Help! Help!' cried Arthur. Servants ran in through all the doors. They pulled Miles from Arthur.

An hour later, Miles and Edward sat on the cold floor of a dark prison.

Chapter 13   Prison

'When will we get out?' asked Edward. 'I have to get to London.'

'We will have to wait for the judge. He will listen to Arthur. I hope that he will listen to me too. Then he will give the house to Arthur or to me. Perhaps he will say we are mad. Perhaps they will send us away.'

'Send me away? The king?' said Edward.

They heard a sound at the door. An old man came in and put some food on the table. He did not look at them, but Miles looked at him.

'Basil? It is Basil!' cried Miles. 'My father's old servant!'

'Is it Mr Miles?' asked the old man. 'But Mr Miles died in France.'

'No, he is not dead. He is standing here in front of you. My brother, Arthur, wrote that letter from France.'

'Oh, Mr Miles, this is wonderful – you are home. Your poor father died only two weeks after that letter came. He was very unhappy. Then your brother sent the old servants away from the House. But now you are here again. Can I tell everybody?'

'No, no!' said Miles. 'Don't tell anybody. Or my brother will kill me when I get out of prison. When I get out, I will go to London. I have friends there. Sir Humphrey Marlow is head of the king's soldiers at Westminster Palace. He was with me in France. He knows me. And other people know me. I will take them to the king. The king will give me my home again. Say nothing, Basil.'

Edward laughed. 'The king! And who is the king, Basil?'

'King Henry is dead,' answered Basil. 'The young Prince Edward is the king. But he is very young – he is only ten years old. It will be difficult for him.'

'We have to get out of this prison!' cried Edward. 'I have to go to London.'

◆

Edward did not have to wait for a long time. The judge came the next day and heard Arthur's story.

'You say that this man is not your brother. Who, then, is he?' he asked.

'I do not know him,' Arthur answered. 'He is a stranger to me. He is a mad beggar. He thinks that he is my brother. But my dear brother Miles died in France. He fought with the king's soldiers and he gave his life for his country. And this boy with the stranger – he is also mad. He thinks that he is the King of England!'

The judge did not listen to Miles's story.

'Arthur Hendon,' he said, 'the house is yours. I do not think that this man is your brother. Nobody knows him. Perhaps he met your brother in France and heard his story. And then your brother died, so he thought of his plan.' But the judge was a kind man and he felt sorry for Miles and Edward. 'Take them away,' he ordered. 'Take them to the town gates. They can go on their way.'

Chapter 14   The New King

When Miles and Edward arrived in London again, there were crowds of people in the streets.

'They want to see their new king,' said Miles.

'And I am here,' said Edward. 'But I cannot go to the palace. The soldiers will not open the gates for me. I have to think of a plan.'

They found a room.

'Sir Miles,' said Edward. 'Bring me a pen and paper. I want to write a letter.'

'Who are you writing to?' asked Miles. He laughed. 'To the king? He won't read letters today. Today he has more important things in his head.'

Edward sat and thought. 'I am king but how can I show them that?' he said. 'What do I know and what does Tom not know?

What does nobody in the world know – only me?...Yes! There is one thing...'

He quickly wrote something down. 'Now,' he said to Miles, let's go to Westminster.'

◆

They quickly came to the gates of Westminster Palace.

Tom was ready in the Great Room, in the prince's finest clothes. The great lords and ladies of England were ready. Lord Hertford and Lord Somerset waited with Tom. At the door stood Sir Humphrey Marlow with his soldiers.

Suddenly there was a loud noise at the gates. Men shouted and fought. Sir Humphrey turned to one of his men. 'What is happening? Go and see,' he said in his ear.

The soldier quickly came back. 'There is a man there with a boy. The man says that he is Miles Hendon. The boy says that he has a letter for the king. But he also says that he *is* the king.'

'Miles Hendon!' said Sir Humphrey. 'I remember him from France. He is a fine soldier and a good man. What is he doing in a fight at the palace gates?'

Tom came to Sir Humphrey. 'Did he say a boy? A boy with a letter?'

'Yes, Your Majesty.'

'Bring them here.'

'But Your Majesty, this is not the time–' Sir Humphrey started to say.

'I am ordering you,' said Tom. 'Bring them to me now. I want to see them.'

So the king's soldiers brought Miles and Edward into the Great Room. When Tom saw Edward, he was very happy. 'Your Majesty!' he cried. 'You are here!'

'He is going mad again,' said Lord Hertford. 'What can we do?'

Edward gave Tom his hand and Tom stood up.

'Take that boy,' Sir Humphrey ordered his soldiers. He looked at Edward.

'Stop!' cried Lord Hertford. 'Look at their faces. They are the same. Which boy is our king? Perhaps our king is *not* mad. Perhaps our king is not the king. Perhaps he really is a pauper.'

Everybody in the Great Room started to talk at the same time.

'What question can we ask them?' said Lord Somerset. 'What question can only Edward answer?'

Lord Hertford turned to Edward. He asked him questions about King Henry, about Edward's mother, about Westminster Palace, about Lady Mary, Lady Elizabeth and Lady Jane. Edward answered the questions.

'But,' said Lord Somerset, 'I can answer those questions too. What does only the king know?'

'Can we read your letter, Your Majesty?' said Tom to Edward.

Edward gave the letter to Lord Hertford. It said, 'Where is the Great Seal?'

Lord Hertford turned to Tom. 'I asked Your Majesty before your father died. You didn't know the answer. Can you tell me the answer now?'

'I don't know the answer because I am not the king. How many times do I have to tell you that?' answered Tom.

'Look under the large cup on the highest shelf in my room,' said Edward. 'You will find it there.'

Lord Hertford left the room. For five minutes everybody waited and nobody spoke. Then they heard Lord Hertford.

'He is right! He is right! I have the Great Seal. The king is the pauper. The pauper is the king.'

And everybody in the room bowed to Edward, their young king. Well, nearly everybody. Miles Hendon stood with his mouth open. He did not bow because he could not move.

Chapter 15   The End

So the story ended happily. Edward was king, not Tom, and he was a very good king. He was a better king because for five days he was a pauper. He knew his people now, after his time with them on the streets of London and in Kent. He knew about their lives, and he understood their problems.

Tom lived in Westminster Palace and he was the king's closest friend. After a long day in the Great Room with Lord Hertford, Edward went into the palace gardens with Tom for an hour.

Miles – now, Sir Miles – went back to Hendon House and married Lady Edith. Arthur had to give back everything and, of course, he got nothing. King Edward often visited Hendon House. Basil was the head gardener there.

Nobody saw John Canty again. Nobody wanted to see him again. Edward gave Tom's mother and sisters a fine house in the country. They studied Latin and French and lived happy lives.

But a sad time followed. Edward died when he was only fifteen.

So Tom moved to the home of his mother and sisters. And there he wrote down the story of the prince and the pauper.

ACTIVITIES

Chapters 1–5

Before you read

1 Look at the pictures in this book. What is this story about?

2 Find these words in your dictionary. They are all in the story.

   ✓*king lady lord pauper prince servant soldier*

   The year is 1537 and the place is England. Who:

   a is the most important person in the country? *king*

   b is his son? *prince*

   c fights for their country? *soldier*

   d has no money? *pauper*

   e works in another person's house? *serant*

   f is a woman from a rich or important family? *lady*

   g is a man from a rich or important family? *lord*

3 Look for these words in your dictionary. Put them in the sentences.

   beg gate mad order palace poor

   a A person with no money has to ..... for food. *beg*

   b He/she is very .... *poor*

   c He/she does not live in a .... *Palace*

   d When the king arrives at the palace, the soldiers open the ...... *gate*

   e When the king gives an ...... to his soldiers, they listen. *order*

   f A poor boy thinks that he is the King of England. He is .... *mad*

4 Now find these words. Answer the questions.

   banquet bow crowd prison seal sword

   a What did people do in front of an important person?

   b Which place can you not walk out of?

   c Which is the word for a great dinner for many people?

   d What did the king use on his letters and papers?

   e What is the word for a lot of people in one place?

   f What can you use when you want to kill somebody?

After you read

5 Edward and Tom want to go back to their old lives. Who does Edward ask for help? Who does Tom ask for help? What can they do?

Chapters 6–10

Before you read

6 Tom is going to a banquet. What do you think will happen there?

After you read

7 Make these sentences right.
   a Tom goes to the Guildhall by road.
   b John Canty kicks Father Andrew to the ground.
   c Tom's old grandmother is very kind.
   d The family take the old grandmother with them when they leave London.
   e John Canty finds Edward in the crowd after he runs away.
   f Miles Hendon fought in France for the French king.
   g Miles Hendon gives Edward orders.

8 In Chapter 10 Tom finds answers to his family's problems in his sleep. Does this happen to you? Discuss this with a friend.

Chapters 11–15

Before you read

9 Miles Hendon wants to go back to Hendon House. Work with another student and have this conversation.
   Student A: You are Miles. When you arrive home, Arthur is in the dining room.
   Student B: You are Arthur, Miles's younger brother. Miles is home after seven years.

10 What is the job of a judge? Find the word *judge* in your dictionary.

After you read

11 Which of the words below can you use when you talk about these
people? You can use each word for different people. You can also
use other words.

Miles   John Canty   Edward   Henry VIII   Lady Jane   Tom
Tom's mother   Tom's grandmother

afraid   angry   beautiful   dangerous   friendly   hard   intelligent
kind   large   nice   rich   poor   strong   stupid

Writing

12 Who would you like to be? Why?

13 Look at Chapter 10 again. You are Tom. It is night time. Make
notes about your day.

14 Look at Chapter 11 again. You were in the town square. Write a
letter to a friend about Edward and the chicken.

15 You are King Edward. This is your first day in the job. What are you
going to do? Think of five things.